W9-BXW-587

Women in
Fashion

BY REBECCA RISSMAN

CONTENT CONSULTANT
Belinda T. Orzada, PhD
Professor, Fashion and Apparel Design
University of Delaware

Essential Library

An Imprint of Abdo Publishing | abdopublishing.com

WOMEN'S LIVES *in* Hisory

abdopublishing.com

Published by Abdo Publishing, a division of ABDO, PO Box 398166, Minneapolis, Minnesota 55439. Copyright © 2017 by Abdo Consulting Group, Inc. International copyrights reserved in all countries. No part of this book may be reproduced in any form without written permission from the publisher. Essential Library™ is a trademark and logo of Abdo Publishing.

Printed in the United States of America, North Mankato, Minnesota
032016
092016

Cover Photo: iStockphoto; Shutterstock Images
Interior Photos: Matteo Prandoni/BFA/Sipa/AP Images, 4–5; David X Prutting/BFAnyc/Sipa USA/Newscom, 7; Sam Aronov/Shutterstock Images, 11; Picture History/Newscom, 13; AP Images, 14–15, 22, 31, 46–47; Photos 12/Alamy, 19; Bettmann/Corbis, 21, 38; Yale Joel/The LIFE Picture Collection/Getty Images, 23; SNAP/REX/Newscom, 24–25; Everett Collection/Shutterstock Images, 27, 28, 80–81; Jacques Brinon/AP Images, 32–33; Alfred T. Palmer NC History Images/Newscom, 34–35; Keystone Archives/Heritage Images/Glow Images, 37, 41; PHOTOPQR/OUEST France/Newscom, 44–45; Arthur Sidey Mirrorpix/Newscom, 51; LAMedia Collection/Sunshine/ZumaPress/Newscom, 53; Janus/ImageBROKER RM/Glow Images, 54; Ingolf Hatz/Cultura RM/Glow Images, 55; Rex Features/Newscom, 56–57; Land of Lost Content/Heritage Images/Glow Images, 59; Lev Radin/Shutterstock Images, 61, 72, 88; Remy de la Mauviniere/AP Images, 64; Barry Sweet/AP Images, 67; ABC/courtesy Everett Collection, 68–69; Ovidiu Hrubaru/Shutterstock Images, 73; Stocklight/Shutterstock Images, 75; Shutterstock Images, 78, 94; Chrystyna Czajkowsky/AP Images, 79; Scott Roth/Invision/AP Images, 83; Nata Sha/Shutterstock Images, 86; Lannis Waters/ZumaPress/Newscom, 90–91; Jae C. Hong/AP Images, 93

Editor: Mirella Miller
Series Designer: Maggie Villaume

Cataloging-in-Publication Data
Names: Rissman, Rebecca, author.
Title: Women in fashion / by Rebecca Rissman.
Description: Minneapolis, MN : Abdo Publishing, [2017] | Series: Women's lives
    in history | Includes bibliographical references and index.
Identifiers: LCCN 2015960318 | ISBN 9781680782912 (lib. bdg.) |
    ISBN 9781680774856 (ebook)
Subjects: LCSH: Fashion--Juvenile literature. | Clothing trade--
    --Juvenile literature. | Entrepreneurship--Juvenile literature. | Women in the
    professions--Juvenile literature.
Classification: DDC 391--dc23
LC record available at http://lccn.loc.gov/2015960318

Contents

Danielle Bernstein attends
a design launch for H&M in
October 2015.

CHAPTER ONE

Modern Fashionistas and Their Historic Roots

W hen Danielle Bernstein posts a selfie to her Instagram account, WeWoreWhat, she is not just showing off her cozy sweater, manicure, and steamy mug of coffee. She is broadcasting a calculated advertising image to more than one million followers who tap her posts to learn where her sweater is from, what color her nail polish is, and where she bought her coffee. Bernstein is part of the new generation of women in fashion. She is not a designer, fashion buyer, or model. She is a blogger in her early 20s garnering tens of thousands of likes per post. And she is making hundreds of thousands of dollars a year.[1]

Bloggers and Instagrammers have a huge impact on the fashion industry. Just by posting photos, they introduce up-and-coming designers to millions of people. They can spread a trend, share a favorite style, or inspire reluctant shoppers to try out a new look. Fashion insiders understand that Instagram and fashion blogs are highly effective visual advertising channels. People browsing on their mobile phones and computers can see clothing, styles, and brands and be inspired to dress differently or buy new garments.

Women occupy a unique niche in the fashion blogosphere. Readers often relate more with female fashion bloggers than with traditional fashion journalists. Unlike fashion writers at magazines such as *Vogue*, who work with famous photographers and models, many bloggers work from home and take photos on their mobile phones. This makes them seem relatable and nonthreatening. Many readers also appreciate the ability to see what clothing looks like on these fashion bloggers, rather than on models. Women like Bernstein have learned to wield online tools such as Instagram to spread their ideas about fashion around the world and make money at the same time.

VOGUE

Vogue magazine began in 1892 as a weekly magazine that focused on the fashion and events of elite New Yorkers. Condé Nast Publishers purchased the magazine in 1909 and shifted its focus to women's fashion. Over the years, *Vogue* has established itself as a tastemaker for its readers and as an outlet for artistic and fashionable expression for designers, models, and photographers. Today, *Vogue* is a successful, globally distributed fashion magazine and website. The magazine is published in 21 international editions that reach 23.5 million readers. Vogue.com reaches millions more each year.[2]

Bernstein, *left*, uses different forms of social media to reach her millions of followers.

Women Making Fashion History

The women who are changing the face of fashion today are very different from the female fashion pioneers of the past. But women have always been instrumental in influencing the colors, cuts, fabrics, and styles of clothing worn by those who could afford to make choices about their wardrobes. Women such as Marie Antoinette, Queen Elizabeth I, and Mary, Queen of Scots, were historical style makers whose royal portraits and appearances dictated what fashionable women should wear and how they should wear it.

FEMALE MINISTER OF FASHION

Rose Bertin was a French dressmaker and milliner. She went on to impact the fashions worn in the highest royal courts around the world. Bertin's bubbly personality and bold design style helped her find her way into the spotlight. She began creating dresses for members of the French court in the late 1760s. She was hired to create a gown for the young queen Marie Antoinette's coronation in 1775, and soon after became the fashionable queen's go-to stylist and friend.

Bertin pioneered several trends for Marie Antoinette, such as high hairstyles, simple muslin country gowns, and formal court dress. The country gowns Marie Antoinette made famous were shockingly casual for a queen. These white dresses were loosely belted and comfortable. The formal gowns Bertin designed for Marie Antoinette were more acceptable for a queen's wardrobe. They were elaborate, stiff, and opulent. They reflected the great wealth and power the French associated with their royalty.

Bertin's close friendship with the queen helped her become a fashion supplier for many members of the royal family and other courtiers. Bertin soon became known as the Minister of Fashion for the French court, which was the pinnacle of glamour at the time. Wealthy women around the world imitated the styles worn there.

These historic female style makers were typically not designers or seamstresses. They had little to do with the construction of their gowns. Rather, they were wealthy women who were able to buy the clothing they wanted. They worked with couturiers, milliners, and other craftspeople to create cutting-edge looks that reflected their values. As time passed, however, women began to play a more involved role in the fashion industry as stylists, dressmakers, and designers.

DRESSMAKING

At the dawn of the 1900s, dressmaking was one of the few jobs considered appropriate for young women outside of the home. Though most clients exercised control over the style of garments they ordered, some dressmakers were able to develop distinct styles. Anna and Laura Tirocchi were well-known dressmakers in Providence, Rhode Island, from 1911 until the 1940s. They worked with clients to adapt styles found in magazines with embellished trims and unique fabrics. Though they did not entirely design the gowns they made, the Tirocchi's had a strong impact on the final outcome of their clients' wardrobes.

Setting the Scene for a Century of Style

In the late 1800s and early 1900s, the fashion industry was blossoming. The first department stores were opening in Paris, France, allowing wealthy women to shop for beautiful, ready-to-wear clothing. For the first time, stores were selling mass-produced clothing. These garments were created in different, distinct sizes. People could simply purchase them and put them on. This was a change from the past, when each garment was custom-sewn according to a client's measurements. Women looking for one-of-a-kind garments were also in luck. Charles Frederick Worth, the man often credited with inventing haute couture, opened his influential studio, House of Worth. Women living outside of Europe did not need to worry about missing out on the fashion trends seen in Paris, France; Rome,

Italy; or London, England. The first fashion magazines, such as *Godey's Lady's Book* and *Peterson's Magazine*, appeared on newsstands and showed fashionable women what looks were popular.

Though many people considered fashion a frivolous pursuit, it was an undeniable element of upper-class life. Even Virginia Woolf, the famous poet, weighed in on the issue: "Vain trifles as they seem, clothes have, they say, more important offices than to merely keep us warm. They change our view of the world and the world's view of us."[3]

Women in Fashion

Women have long held important roles in the fashion industry. In the years before women were free to pursue careers in fashion as designers, they still shaped the way people dressed. Some wealthy aristocratic women did this by patronizing designers who allowed them to collaborate on looks. Others made bold choices from within their own wardrobes, creating innovative ensembles from existing pieces. Still other women acted as muses for designers. These women inspired designers to create

THE BEAUTY OF THE BELLE ÉPOQUE

At the beginning of the 1900s, fashionable men and women enjoyed a time known as the Belle Époque, which means the "beautiful age."[4] Leisure activities such as dancing and swimming were popular pursuits amongst the wealthy classes. One woman came to embody the spirit of the age with her graceful beauty. Cléo de Mérode was a Parisian ballet dancer whose style became more famous than her dancing. Mérode wore her hair in a low bun with the sides covering her ears. She often wore embellished headbands across her forehead to accent this look. Women all around Paris imitated the style of the woman nicknamed "the beauty of the Belle Époque."[5] Artists noticed her too. Henri de Toulouse-Lautrec and Alexandre Falguière both created art in her likeness. Mérode's image was even printed on postcards.

garments that matched or complemented their personalities.

Today, women have taken over the fashion industry in large numbers. Female models, designers, stylists, and art directors are constantly shaping the fashion industry. Women hold some of the highest offices within fashion empires, are groundbreaking designers, spread trends, and dictate styles.

Understanding the rise of women in the fashion industry involves learning about the evolving role of gender in the 1900s. At the outset of the 1900s, women had few rights and were expected to conform to rigid cultural standards. Through decades of work, though, women slowly gained the freedom to work, live, and express themselves. Today, this freedom is evident in countless aspects of modern life. But it is visibly evident in fashion. Modern women

New York Fashion Week is a time each year when designers showcase their new work.

THE ORIGINAL "IT GIRL"

In 1900, Evelyn Nesbit moved to New York City to become an artist's model. Before long, though, she started getting work posing for fashion photographers and magazine illustrators. She added stage work to her career, becoming a chorus girl in the successful musical *Florodora* at the age of 16. Soon, she was an icon of the age. Famed illustrator Charles Dana Gibson immortalized Nesbit in his famous Gibson Girl drawings that appeared in magazines such as *Harper's Magazine* and *Life*. These drawings captured the ideal American woman of the time, with an hourglass figure, perfectly coiffed hair, and sophisticated attitude.

incorporate fashion into their lives as an element of self-expression, power, and identity. As designer Anne Klein put it, "Clothes aren't going to change the world. The women who wear them will."[6]

Amelia Bloomer

In 1849, US women's rights activist Amelia Bloomer founded a New York newspaper called *The Lily*. The small paper focused on issues that affected women, such as voting rights and the dangers of alcohol.

One issue Bloomer tackled in her paper was women's dress reform. She believed the garments women were expected to wear, such as corsets and petticoats, were too restricting. Instead, Bloomer suggested that women dress for a more active lifestyle. In 1851, she proposed a new style of dress for women, with loose tops and knee-length skirts worn over pants. Though Bloomer was widely mocked for wearing the style that would soon be named after her, she maintained that women welcomed the change in traditional style: "As soon as it became known that I was wearing the new dress, letters came pouring in upon me by the hundreds from women all over the country making inquiries about the dress and asking for patterns—showing how ready and anxious women were to throw off the burden of long, heavy skirts."[7]

(1818–1894)

Queen Victoria shocked a nation by wearing a nontraditional white wedding gown.

CHAPTER TWO

New Styles for a New World

When Queen Victoria of Britain wed Prince Albert in 1840, she shocked English aristocratic circles with her gown. Rather than wearing red, the traditional choice for royal brides, the 20-year-old fashion-forward young woman walked down the aisle wearing the historic color of mourning: white. Since the young queen was not in mourning, this was very confusing for people. It was not only the color she chose that opposed tradition. Victoria also decided not to wear the expected velvet robes lined with ermine, the rich fur associated with royalty. Instead of a diamond crown, she wore a simple crown made from orange blossoms.

The shock waves from this ensemble did not last. In fact, it was not long before English brides began to imitate Queen Victoria's style. Critics even began to look for symbolism in the color white. Less than ten years after Victoria shocked fashion fans with her white dress, *Godey's Lady's Book* declared that it had always been the right choice for brides:

"Custom has decided, from the earliest ages, that white is the most fitting hue, whatever may be the material. It is an emblem of the purity and innocence of girlhood, and the unsullied heart she now yields to the chosen one."[1] The impact of Victoria's white dress has been lasting. Today, the white dress remains an iconic part of Western wedding ceremonies.

Queen Victoria would go on to start many other fashion trends during her reign. Her preferences shaped the way women wore their hair, jewelry, and makeup. When Prince Albert died in 1861, Queen Victoria's commitment to wearing mourning clothing even became a fashion trend.

New Century, New Styles

The first two decades of the 1900s were marked by transition, growth, and change. Huge political events changed the way people lived around the globe. World War I (1914–1918) was fought mostly in Europe, Africa, and Asia, but battles of this epic war were fought on every continent except Antarctica and took the lives of more than nine million men.[2] Even after the end of the war, Americans continued to experience enormous changes. In 1920, after decades of

CLOCHE HATS

Caroline Reboux was a Parisian milliner. Her most famous creation sparked one of the biggest hat trends of the 1920s. Reboux made a close-fitting bell-shaped hat called a cloche hat. This cap was especially popular because of the way it complemented the short hairstyles of the time. In addition to her cloche hats, she became known for making quality hats that were tastefully adorned with feathers.

work by activists, women finally gained the right to vote.

These years were full of cultural change too. Jazz exploded onto the music scene, bringing with it a new crowd of fashionable tastemakers. Musicians, dancers, artists, and young aristocrats started dictating what was in style. Flappers, the nickname given to young, stylish women, began to shape the standards of beauty. Gone were the upswept hairstyles, cinched waists, and elaborate gowns with full skirts. Flappers replaced them with short hair, straight dresses that ended at the knee, and boyish silhouettes. They embraced anything that looked modern. Jazz stars such as Josephine Baker embodied this new, unique glamour.

Paris was at the epicenter of fashion during the first years of the 1900s. Both department stores and high fashion were born there. Though there were many men influencing Parisian style, these years were also heavily influenced by female designers.

BYE BYE, BINDING CORSETS!

In the early 1900s, women still wore binding corsets under their dresses. These stiff, restricting undergarments helped women achieve specific silhouettes that were considered fashionable. Women wore corsets that gave them extreme hourglass figures, with tiny waists and exaggerated hips. After the hourglass silhouette came the S shape. Women wore corsets that pushed their hips and bottoms back and their chests up and forward, giving them an S-shaped silhouette.

When the 1920s rolled around, women were tired of the constricting nature of binding corsets. A more active lifestyle made these undergarments especially unappealing. Many also believed the long-term effects of extremely tight corsets were unhealthy. They worried that binding the organs and ribs would be harmful for women. Flappers were among the first to cast aside their old corsets in favor of softer undergarments.

Jeanne Paquin: The Master of Marketing

Paris was the perfect place for budding designers at the dawn of the 1900s. It was a freethinking city with an appreciation for art and beauty. One designer who shaped many aspects of the fashion industry was Jeanne Paquin. She started her career as a dressmaker living in Paris. After developing her own sense of style, she opened her studio, Maison Paquin. She became famous for tastefully accenting coats and other garments with fur, lining black overcoats with bright fabric, and embellishing dark gowns with lace or other trims.

One of Paquin's greatest innovations was in the way she marketed her fashions. She would dress beautiful models in her fashions and then send them to stylish parties or trendy locales,

TRIANGLE SHIRTWAIST FIRE

In the early 1900s, many garment workers labored in sweatshops to mass-produce the ready-to-wear clothing so many consumers wanted. These factories often required laborers to work long hours in poor conditions for very low wages.

In 1911, more than 600 people worked at the Triangle Shirtwaist Company, a factory in New York City. The employees were mostly women who had recently immigrated to the United States. They spoke little English and had few rights as workers.

When the eighth floor of the factory caught fire on March 25, a disaster ensued. Employees frantically tried to break through doors that had been locked to prevent employee theft. The fire hoses, which managers used in an attempt to control the flames, were old and ineffective. Before the day was over, 145 people had died in the fire. Of those who lost their lives, 129 were women.[3]

This horrible incident raised awareness of the poor conditions faced by many workers in the garment industry. Shortly after the fire, 80,000 people marched to protest the conditions in factories.[4] Later, the Ladies Garment Workers Union was formed, which helped prevent future disasters by advocating for better working conditions in the United States. It also helped raise awareness of the inequalities faced by women working in the garment industry.

such as the horse races at Longchamp and Chantilly. Her unconventional marketing methods worked. She accumulated some of the most desirable customers of the day, including royalty, film stars, and the wives of US business tycoons, including the Astors and the Rockefellers. Paquin even became the first Parisian designer to branch out, opening foreign studios in Madrid, Spain; Buenos Aires, Argentina; and London, England.

From Children's Clothing to Couture

While Paquin was innovating the way fashion was marketed, another female designer in Paris was working to change the way people thought of fashion altogether. Jeanne Lanvin was a talented designer who started her career as a milliner. After she had

Embellishments were often added to Paquin's designs.

her daughter Marguerite in 1897, she began sewing fashionable clothing for the young girl. Soon, people were requesting that Lanvin sew clothing for their own children. It was not long before Lanvin was creating unique clothing for both children and adults. In 1909, she officially opened her own studio, where she designed gowns for princesses, actresses, and other prominent women. She became known for expertly crafting beautiful gowns out of soft, flowing fabrics such as silk. She also had an eye for color and favored a bold blue, which came to be known as "Lanvin blue."[5] Her chemise-style dresses became favorites among flappers, who enjoyed the way these dresses hung straight down in a column but left their lower legs free. Lanvin's decorations of beads and sequins made these dresses especially appropriate for nights spent dancing to jazz. The embellishments flashed and bounced along with the dancers, making for a dazzling sight on the dance floor.

Lanvin did not only produce beautiful garments for women and children. She also pioneered the notion of fashion as a lifestyle. Her fashion house was the first to sell lifestyle goods, such as fragrances, men's clothing, and home design. The House of Lanvin, one of the oldest continuously run fashion houses in France, remains a staple in high fashion circles today. Celebrities can often be spotted in Lanvin gowns on red carpets and at elite events.

Coco Chanel and Her Glamorous Legacy

The hard work of Paquin and Lanvin paved the way for female designers who would follow them. One of the most famous designers in the history of fashion, Coco Chanel, entered the fashion world in the early 1900s and forever changed the industry. Chanel would go on to define high-class glamour and style for wealthy women in Paris and around the world. Her most iconic fashion creations were the Chanel suit with the collarless jacket created in 1925, the little black dress in 1926, and the idea that luxury must be comfortable.

Many of Lanvin's designs used flowing fabrics for added comfort for the wearer.

Chanel learned how to sew in the orphanage where she grew up.

Chanel began her career in fashion as a milliner. She opened her first hat shop in Paris in 1910 and soon added more stores to her franchise. She began selling women's clothing, including a soft jersey dress that made her styles very popular. In the 1920s, she created her famous perfume, Chanel No. 5.

Chanel's impact on the fashion world was lasting. She encouraged women to be unique and to follow their own hearts, especially when it came to style. Chanel once reminded women of this, saying, "In order to be irreplaceable one must always be different."[7] The women who followed Chanel into the world of fashion design clearly listened to her advice. At the dawn of the 1930s, women brought new and fresh ideas into fashion design, even during a time of great turmoil.

Caresse Crosby

Caresse Crosby, a wealthy socialite living in New York City in the early 1900s, got tired of wearing constricting undergarments—so she invented the modern bra. Using two handkerchiefs, ribbons, pins, and a sense of ingenuity, Crosby created a lightweight and comfortable garment she called the backless brassiere. She patented her creation in 1914, and soon after started her own business to sell the groundbreaking garment. She called her company the Fashion Form Brassiere Company. It was very successful, and eventually she sold her patent to the Warner Brothers Corset Company.

Crosby was not just an innovator in the world of fashion. She and her second husband, Harry Crosby, founded a publishing house in Paris and went on to publish works by famous authors such as James Joyce.

(1891–1970)

Jean Harlow's fashion choices were much different from what the rest of the country could afford in the 1930s.

CHAPTER THREE

The Thrilling 1930s

Jean Harlow shocked 1930s moviegoers with her seductive looks and scandalous styles. She wore revealing, form-fitting silk dresses and a short, platinum blonde bob. Harlow's fashion was glamorous and high maintenance in a time when few Americans had the money or the time to spend on their clothes. But that did not stop the screen star from inspiring a generation of women to go blonde and experiment with daring dresses.

In the 1930s, life in the United States changed drastically. A series of economic disasters rocked the country, and people everywhere were scrambling to make enough money to pay for food and housing. In 1929, the stock market crashed, causing investors to lose billions of dollars. This disastrous event marked the beginning of the Great Depression, the worst financial crisis in the history of the Western world. Then, a devastating drought hit the Midwest. Agriculture and livestock farmers suffered terrible losses. The drought lasted three years and caused horrible dust storms. Soon, this period of time became known as the Dust Bowl.

In the midst of the economic struggles of the 1930s, fashion and beauty seemed like frivolous pursuits. Few Americans were able to afford nice clothing or expensive beauty treatments. Those who could afford these luxuries had to be discreet so as not to offend the masses of poor and needy people. But this did not mean Americans were no longer interested in fashion and beauty. The very wealthy still bought fine fashions and spent time at beauty retreats and spas. Middle- and lower-class Americans who could not indulge in fashions themselves simply had to look elsewhere to get their beauty fix. Many Americans looked across the Atlantic Ocean to Paris, which was widely accepted as the center of high fashion. Others found inspiration closer to home in US cinema. Though most Americans could not afford fashionable garments, film stars were seen as icons of high style and glamour. Looking at the fashions of the rich

THE 1939 WORLD'S FAIR

The 1939 New York World's Fair was an important event for the fashion industry. The fair featured The Hall of Fashion, a venue that showcased the advances Americans had made in textiles and clothing construction. It also featured fashion shows that highlighted the work of US fashion designers.

The fair was also an important place for influential women in fashion to see and be seen. Film star Marlene Dietrich stunned crowds in her elegant turban and voluminous fur coat. The First Lady, Eleanor Roosevelt, also wowed onlookers with her long-sleeved printed dress and matching hat. Famous ballerina Vera Zorina inspired fashion-forward women with her printed dress, wide-brimmed hat, and fur scarf.

and famous on screen, in magazines, and on the news gave the masses a chance to imagine what luxurious life might be like. Glamorous events such as the World's Fair of 1939 provided average people with the chance to witness the lives and styles of the very wealthy.

As it had been in previous decades, hat making continued to be a gateway for women to enter into the fashion world. Many women started their careers crafting unique hats before expanding their businesses to include other garments. Hats, after all, were an important part of fashion for both men and women. As more and more people faced financial restrictions due to the depression, hats were an affordable fashion item. Women who could not afford to purchase a new dress could, and often did, buy hats as a way to refresh their wardrobe.

After a tough end to the 1920s, many Americans imagined having the life and wardrobe of movie stars.

Hats were important fashion accessories during the 1930s.

JOAN CRAWFORD'S PUFFED SLEEVES

In 1932, film and fashion star Joan Crawford appeared in a movie called *Letty Lynton* wearing a white chiffon gown with huge puffed sleeves. The dress was designed to mask Crawford's unusually broad shoulders, but it created an instant fashion craze in the United States. Macy's department store claimed it sold 500,000 replicas of the dress after the film's release. *Vogue* magazine reported the country was awash with "little Joan Crawfords."[1]

Schiaparelli's "Shocking Pink"

One designer who achieved success in this difficult climate was Italian-born Elsa Schiaparelli. As a young woman, she lived in some of the world's most fashionable cities: Rome, London, and New York City. Finally, she moved to Paris, where she met the extremely successful designer Paul Poiret. She charmed the fashion visionary, and he soon allowed her to borrow some of his exclusive and extremely expensive designs to wear around the city. Under Poiret's mentorship, Schiaparelli began crafting her own clothing. She created a simple knit sweater with a trompe l'oeil undershirt design that made it look as though the wearer had a white blouse under a black sweater. The design was an instant success. In 1927, she opened her own design house, Maison Schiaparelli, and in 1934 became the first female designer to appear on the cover of *Time* magazine. Schiaparelli earned a reputation for creating avant-garde fashions and dressing famous actresses, and she was even credited with inventing the color "shocking pink."[2]

Schiaparelli's fashions were heavily influenced by the art and politics of the era. She collaborated with surrealist artists such as Salvador Dalí. Surrealism was an artistic movement that encouraged people to unlock the power and creativity of the unconscious mind. It was a jarring departure from previous artistic styles. In 1937, the duo worked together to create an evening gown with an enormous

WOMEN MILLINERS

Hats were important accessories for fashionable women in the 1930s. Many women fashion designers got their start working as milliners. They crafted unique designs from felt, silk, wool, and even straw, and added flowers, fur, and feathers as embellishments.

One hat designer who stood out during this time was Lilly Daché. In the 1930s, she was famous for creating chic and trendy turbans. She often crafted them directly onto her clients' heads by draping and wrapping fabric. Her clients included rich and famous members of high society and film stars. One of her most famous fans was actress Marlene Dietrich.

lobster painted on the front. The unusual dress was fascinating to lovers of fashion and art. *Vogue* magazine even featured it in an eight-page spread.

When World War II (1939–1945) broke out in Europe, Schiaparelli kept her fashion house open and made clothing that reflected the political turmoil of the era. She famously said, "In difficult times, fashion is always outrageous."[3] She created unique war-inspired garments, such as a zippered jumpsuit that could be worn while running for shelter during an air raid. She also created a coat that contained an integrated handbag, so that women did not have to stop to grab their purse in an emergency. Schiaparelli believed fashion was an art form that reflected the world around it.

Madeleine Vionnet and the Bias Cut

Another woman who achieved success in the 1930s was Madeleine Vionnet. She was widely credited with inventing the bias cut, a diagonal way of cutting fabric that allows it to stretch and move easily. Cutting fabric on a bias made dresses more fluid and comfortable. It also made them more body-hugging and revealing. This marked a huge departure from the often stiff, constricting styles

Elsa Schiaparelli looks
through new designs
in Paris in 1949.

Transparences

of other designers. In addition to being a master of draping and fitting the body, Vionnet was influential because of the way her clothing reflected the changing role of women in society. Her gowns did not require stiff, binding corsets. In fact, corsets ruined the shape of her dresses. Her flowing, Greek-inspired frocks allowed women's bodies to move naturally. Vionnet broke with historical tradition by allowing a woman's personality and interests to define the way they dressed. She often said, "When a woman smiles, then her dress should smile too."[5]

Vionnet was an enormous success. She maintained her fashion studio on the prestigious Avenue Montaigne in Paris beginning in 1912. This street was known as one of the most elite places for the most famous and coveted designers of the time. Maison Vionnet was known as the "temple of fashion."[6] Vionnet finally closed her studio in 1939, at the age of 63, when World War II threatened life and business in Europe.

Women of the Thirties

The thirties might have been a decade of change and challenge for many, but women still managed to leave their mark on the fashions of the time. These artists and entrepreneurs rose above economic challenges to express their thoughts and creative vision through clothing. Female film stars, dancers, dressmakers, socialites, and designers all influenced the way women dressed. They also inspired the fashion stars of the years to come.

Clothing in the 1940s reflected the changing times of women working in factory jobs.

CHAPTER FOUR

The War Years

In 1942, a US power company created a poster that featured a woman wearing a red bandana in her hair and a men's style blue work shirt. Under a banner reading We Can Do It, the model stares at the viewer as she rolls up her sleeve and shows her muscles.

The woman on this poster would later be known as Rosie the Riveter, a popular propaganda character that appeared throughout World War II. This was part of the US government's efforts to recruit women to join the workforce. At the time, most women did not work outside of the home. Unlike stylish women of the past, Rosie did not look weak or frail. She looked strong and vibrant. This new take on beauty would impact the fashion of the 1940s, 1950s, and beyond.

A World at War

In 1939, Nazi Germany invaded Poland, and the world plunged into another colossal conflict as World War II began. The United States joined the war in 1941 after Japanese fighter pilots attacked Pearl Harbor, a US naval base in Hawaii. By the time the war ended, more than 45 million people around the world had been killed.[1] World War II had an enormous impact on the way people lived. This brutal and large-scale conflict made pursuits such as high fashion seem silly and unimportant. In fact, people living in the United Kingdom began referring to the simple, functional clothing styles of the day as civilian clothing 1941, or CC41. The days of beautiful silk gowns and feathered caps were a distant memory.

The war years were hard on Americans. Shortages and rations meant people were unable to buy new items made from valuable materials such as metal or rubber. They had to conserve these resources for the troops fighting abroad. Women entered the workforce in large numbers to replace the millions of men who were sent overseas to fight in the war. Fashion reflected the new, active role women were playing in society. Boxy, practical skirt suits in dark colors, such as brown or green, were popular. Shirtwaist dresses, trousers, and sensible shoes became favorites for working women.

Men serving abroad saw a different side of women's fashion. Voluptuous models wearing skirts, bathing suits, and tight dresses appeared on postcards, posters, and magazine centerfolds. These pinup models wore glamorous and revealing fashions that were rarely seen on women at home. Curvy film actresses such as Marilyn Monroe and Betty Grable were famous, not just for their stylish outfits, but also for their sex appeal.

A Wartime Designer

One designer managed to find enormous success during the difficult war years by creatively manipulating wartime rations and by making military trends stylish. Claire McCardell was a US-born

Fashion in the 1940s was simple
and practical.

McCardell drapes fabric over a
mannequin to create a tailored dress.

woman who created several popular looks during the 1940s and 1950s. Her wraparound, practical denim design could be worn over clothing so women could perform manual labor without ruining their nice dresses. McCardell also integrated adjustable elements such as drawstrings and belts into her clothing, which helped them to fit many different body types.

McCardell pioneered US ready-to-wear clothing. This meant she created garments in different sizes that did not need to be tailored to fit a specific person's body. Ready-to-wear clothing already existed in Europe at the time, but it was called pret-a-porter. McCardell's US translation of this concept was practical, sensible, and relatively affordable. Her Popover dress was available for $6.95 in 1942.[2] This is equivalent to approximately $105 today.[3]

McCardell enjoyed a tremendously successful career. She was the first fashion designer to be voted one of the United States' Women of Achievement. In 1950, President Harry S. Truman awarded her the Women's National Press Club award, a prestigious title given to professional women.

Fashion in Film

Despite facing hardships during the war, many women still emerged as style makers and leaders in the fashion world. Hollywood continued to spread fashion trends with glamorous film wardrobes.

Most Hollywood costume designers during this time were men, but a few women managed to break into this coveted role. One costume designer who was enormously successful was Edith Head. She dressed starlets in films such as *Roman Holiday* and *All About Eve.*

Head became a Hollywood legend. She worked on more than 1,000 films in her career, at both Paramount Pictures and

BETTY GRABLE AND PINUP FASHION

Pinup girls were the models on posters, postcards, and magazine spreads whose images were so popular they were often "pinned up" on the walls of military barracks for soldiers to enjoy. Pinup girls often wore daring and revealing clothing. One of the most popular pinup models from the war years was actress Betty Grable. A 1943 pinup photo of Grable earned itself the title "the picture that launched a million dreams" when it became the most requested photo by military personnel.[4] In it, Grable looks seductively over her shoulder while wearing a light bathing suit and metallic high heels.

Other pinup models also achieved icon status during the war years as men clamored to hang the photos near their bunks. The clothing the models wore in these images came to be almost as well known as the models themselves. Lana Turner wore a tight sweater in hers, earning her the nickname "the sweater girl." Dorothy Lamour's patterned strapless dress earned her pinup photo the title "the sarong."[5]

Universal Studios. From Ingrid Bergman's masculine-styled suits in the 1946 film *Notorious* to Audrey Hepburn's girlish frocks in the 1953 film *Roman Holiday*, Head's stylings were iconic and noteworthy. By the time she retired, she had been nominated for 35 Academy Awards and won a record-breaking eight.[6]

Starlet Style

Many film actresses in the 1940s and 1950s were not in control of their own wardrobes. Studio executives dictated what they wore both on and off screen. Despite this, their names were still associated with the clothes they wore in their films.

One actress who refused to be controlled was Katharine Hepburn. She worked with costume designers to create beautiful, comfortable ensembles for her on-screen roles. Head once commented on the unusual role Hepburn played in dictating her on-screen appearance. "One does not design for Miss Hepburn," she said. "One designs with her."[7] Offscreen, the actress was even more unusual.

Audrey Hepburn

In the 1950s, it was hard to find a bigger celebrity than Audrey Hepburn. Starring in films such as *Roman Holiday*, Hepburn was the ultimate Hollywood darling. Her performances earned her Emmy, Tony, Grammy, and Academy Awards. And her stylish appearances earned her a place in the International Best-Dressed List's Hall of Fame in 1961.

Hepburn's thick eyebrows and boyish frame made her an unlikely style icon, especially given the number of curvy starlets gaining fame at the time. However, her confidence, sense of humor, and distinct ideas about how to dress resonated with women around the world. She became known for looking glamorous and refined on-screen and casual and comfortable in real life. Hepburn started a huge craze by wearing a classic little black dress in *Breakfast at Tiffany's*. She also inspired women to dress in casual capri pants and flats after photographers captured images of the young actress sporting this simple look on the set of her film *Sabrina*.

(1929–1993)

Instead of conforming to mainstream style, Hepburn sported a casual wardrobe of trousers and old sweaters.

New Careers for Women

Fashion photography emerged as an artistic field in Paris in the 1930s. At the time, most fashion photographers were men. But in the 1940s, women started to enter the profession. Lillian Bassman was a former fashion illustrator and textiles designer who made waves as a fashion photographer. Her dramatic fashion photos appeared in *Harper's Bazaar* from the 1940s until the 1960s, making her one of the most well-known female photographers of the time.

Fashion journalism also became a mainstream genre during this time period. When *New York Times* writer Virginia Pope first began reporting on Paris fashions in the 1930s, some readers were surprised. But by the mid-1940s, writers around the world were following her lead. Pope enjoyed working as the *New York Times'* fashion editor between 1933 and 1955. During that time, she revolutionized

WOMEN WEAR PANTS

In the 1930s and early 1940s, a few fashion-forward women, such as Marlene Dietrich and Katharine Hepburn, dared to wear trousers. Many people were shocked to see these masculine garments on such beautiful screen sirens.

As World War II brought women into the workforce in large numbers, more and more women began wearing pants on the job. They were practical and comfortable, and they provided protection in factory work. However, despite the comfort and functionality of pants, most women still preferred to wear skirts and dresses for social outings.

the way people wrote and thought about fashion shows. Thanks to Pope's pioneering work, fashion journalists began reporting on fashion collections in the same way they wrote about other cultural events of note. Pope, along with other female trailblazers writing at *Vogue* and *Harper's Bazaar*, helped make fashion journalism a legitimate, interesting, and profitable career.

From Frills to Another War

In the late 1940s, a brief fashion trend celebrated peacetime with extremely feminine, floral, and frilly dresses. Pioneered by male fashion designer Christian Dior, it was called the New Look. Women wearing the New Look favored full skirts, cinched waists, and fitted bodices. The New Look created an exaggerated hourglass silhouette. Even though this look was wildly popular at the time, these frilly

WOMEN AND THE NEW LOOK

During World War II, women grew accustomed to wearing functional, comfortable attire. Trousers and work shirts made sensible outfits for working women. For footwear, women gave up their high heels and wore durable, comfortable shoes that could withstand long walks and grueling shifts of factory work. This way of dressing sent a message to the world that women were not only mothers and wives; they were also workers. It was a powerful visual representation of a woman's changing role in society.

Christian Dior's New Look challenged the notion that women could be functional laborers. By dressing women in restrictive, frilly, and often-impractical dresses, his styles sent women a message that they were expected to act feminine. His tight frocks required stiff undergarments and were often paired with uncomfortable stilettos. Women wearing the New Look could not work at a factory. To many, the emergence of the New Look meant that women were expected to leave their jobs and return to the home.

Christian Dior's New Look fashions were popular during the late 1940s.

peacetime frocks did not stay fashionable for long. Dior's New Look fell out of fashion after the 1950s.

Just six years after the end of World War II, the United States went to war again. This time, the conflict was the Korean War (1950–1953). Though this war was shorter and involved far fewer casualties, it still affected life for people at home. When the war ended, approximately five million soldiers and civilians had been killed.[9] Just as it had during World War II, women's fashion reflected the war by becoming simpler and less feminine.

The war years were hard on people around the world. But the troubles of these tumultuous years did not stop the evolution of fashion. People needed to wear clothes, and they wanted to enjoy their clothes. Women played an important role in these uncertain decades, as consumers, creators, models, and observers of fashion.

Twiggy was an iconic model
during the 1960s.

CHAPTER FIVE

The Startling 1960s

I n the 1950s, most female beauty icons were curvy and voluptuous women, such as Bettie Page and Marilyn Monroe. But the modern culture of the swinging sixties changed all of that. When a thin, wide-eyed model named Lesley Lawson earned the title The Face of 1966 from British paper the *Daily Express*, it marked a transition into a new era of fashion.[1] Lawson, otherwise known as Twiggy, was the new standard for beauty.

With her boyish haircut, heavily made-up eyes, and scandalously short skirts, Twiggy became the face of a generation. Her fresh look appealed to women who were tired of the overly feminized styles of the past. Twiggy was popular and wildly successful. She appeared on the covers of many fashion magazines, such as *Elle* and *Vogue*. Following her career as a young model, she went on to develop her own clothing line. She also inspired many

ANDY WARHOL AND EDIE SEDGWICK

Edie Sedgwick was a wealthy and troubled socialite from California. In 1964, she moved to New York City to become a model and artist. While in New York, she met Andy Warhol, a famous artist who ran a studio he called the Factory. The Factory was a popular hangout for artists and musicians at the time. It churned out pieces of pop art, such as silkscreen copies of Warhol's famous Campbell's Soup paintings, at a quick rate for eager customers.

Warhol found Sedgwick to be fascinating and entrancing. She was beautiful and had a unique sense of style. She wore heavy eye makeup, extremely short dresses, and long earrings that often dangled to her shoulders. Sedgwick wore her hair in a short, daring bob. Though Warhol was gay, he said his feelings toward her were "probably very close to a certain kind of love."[2] He incorporated her into much of his art, including paintings and films.

artists of the time, including Andy Warhol, who portrayed her likeness in paintings and screen prints.

A Time of Change

The 1960s were a time of enormous change and innovation. The Vietnam War (1955–1975) divided the nation, highlighting the antiwar sentiments of hippies. The civil rights movement worked to gain freedoms for all Americans, especially Americans of color. And the women's liberation movement raised awareness of the inequalities faced by women. All of these changes were reflected in the wide variety of fashion trends that emerged during the 1960s, such as protest fashion and miniskirts. The decade ended with Woodstock, an enormous music festival that celebrated hippie culture, free thinkers, peace, love, and rock and roll.

Women especially experienced huge changes during the 1960s. At the outset of the decade, women lived very sheltered lives. They were expected to raise children, care for their husbands, and keep their homes nice and clean. As the decade progressed and women began to push against these cultural restrictions to pursue their own interests, they met many obstacles. Women could not get credit cards without their husbands' permission. They could not attend universities such as Harvard, Princeton, or Yale. And they had few rights and little equality in the workplace. Their clothing reflected this repression.

As the 1960s bloomed, women's fashions changed dramatically. In the early 1960s, many women still wore the stiff, restrictive, and feminine housedresses that were popular in the late 1950s. However, as more women began to fight for independence and equality in the women's liberation movement, they began to dress differently. Cinched waists and tight girdles were replaced by boxy shift dresses and miniskirts. Delicate floral patterns were tossed aside in favor of electric colors and bold, blocky designs. Women were dressing in a way that told people they were ready for the new generation of equality, women's rights, and new freedoms. This style was known as *mod*, which was short for "modern." Mod style was new, fresh, and exciting.

PROTEST FASHION

The Vietnam War was an extremely divisive conflict for Americans. Many young people did not believe the United States should be participating in the conflict. They protested the war in huge gatherings and marches. These protests were a place for young people to exchange ideas about politics, war, and philosophy. They were also a birthplace for many fashion trends.

At antiwar protests, it was common to see both men and women wearing pieces of military uniforms. The wide-legged pants from naval uniforms were a popular choice. Women wearing them did so as a way to protest old stereotypes about how women should dress and behave. Wearing men's pants made a statement that these women were not interested in conforming to the old idea of femininity. Naval trousers soon inspired other types of wide-legged pants, and before long, the famous bell-bottom pants were born.

WOMEN'S LIBERATION AND THE CIVIL RIGHTS MOVEMENT

In the 1960s, many women began to protest the different ways they were oppressed. One way they did this was by forming women's liberation and feminist groups that worked to fight the inequality they faced in the workplace. Women wanted to be able to work in the same jobs as men and to earn the same wages.

While women were struggling for workplace equality, people of color in the United States were also struggling. The civil rights movement was a campaign that worked to gain all Americans political and social equality, regardless of their race. The women's liberation movement and the civil rights movement had many goals in common, and activists in both groups worked together to try to gain equality for all Americans.

In 1964, activists celebrated Title VII of the Civil Rights Act. This made it illegal to discriminate against someone because of "race, color, religion, sex, or national origin."[4] This monumental law protected the rights of women and people of color, and it opened the door for many female professionals in the 1960s, including fashion designers, photographers, journalists, and models.

Musicians and Miniskirts

One female designer who left her mark on this exciting time was Barbara Hulanicki. She started her career as a fashion illustrator, but after designing an enormously popular pink plaid dress, she opened a fashion boutique in London called Biba. This popular boutique specialized in daring ensembles, such as bright velvet dresses, bold patterned dresses, and floppy hats. One day in 1966, Hulanicki received a box of skirts from a manufacturer that had accidently shrunk. Hulanicki remembered this moment, saying, "I nearly had a heart attack. The skirts were only 10 inches (25 cm) long. 'God,' I thought, 'we'll go bust—we'll never be able to sell them."[3] Luckily for Hulanicki, the skirts were a hit. Customers loved the extra-short and extra-daring

A group of women visit Barbara Hulanicki's shop Biba in London.

skirts. Today, Hulanicki is one of the women credited with the biggest fashion craze of the decade: the miniskirt.

Biba became a hot spot for groundbreaking musicians, artists, and actors. Hulanicki often hosted people such as Twiggy and popular songwriter Marianne Faithfull in her shop. Hulanicki's sense of fashion influenced the way these celebrities dressed and helped to define the rock-star style of the 1960s.

Creating the Chelsea Look

While Hulanicki was busy entertaining celebrities in her boutique, another female fashion leader was busy across town. Mary Quant was a fixture of the London fashion scene in the 1960s. She got her start buying fashions for her small boutique called Bazaar, located in a part of London called Chelsea. When she could not find the clothing she wanted, she decided to make it herself. Her fashions were instantly popular and soon earned the nickname "the Chelsea look" and "the London look."[5] Quant created ensembles with white plastic lace-up knee-high boots and boldly striped sweaters. She also designed shiny plastic raincoats and boldly patterned tights. Quant's customers loved her styles, but they requested that she make her skirts and dresses shorter. She complied, and before long, her name became associated with the famous miniskirts.

Leading Ladies in the Fashion World

Not all of the female fashion pioneers of the 1960s were designers. Actresses, singers, models, and political figures also impacted the way women dressed. First Lady Jacqueline Kennedy inspired US women to wear suits, matching hats, and pearl necklaces. Her teased hairstyle and subtle sense of glamour represented high style in the early years of the decade, before the women's liberation movement had taken off.

Musical acts also inspired the fashion world. The chart-topping musical group The Supremes brought glamour and excess into

JANIS JOPLIN

Janis Joplin was an unconventional singer and songwriter who dominated the airwaves in the 1960s. Fans loved both her husky voice and dynamic performance style. Her confidence and flamboyance went against the cultural stereotypes about female performers, who were expected to act more feminine and refined.

Joplin's sense of style had a huge impact on the decade. Early in her career, she had little money, so she invented an eclectic wardrobe from thrift store purchases, homemade items, and men's clothing. She often topped off her look with oversized sunglasses. As she gained success, Joplin began wearing more elaborate clothing such as velvet capes and fur-lined jackets. She piled on necklaces, bracelets, and rings. Joplin's whimsical, comfortable, and extraordinary sense of style inspired women to dress in similar ways. By the late 1960s, it was a popular way for women and men to dress.

The Supremes were fashion icons and role models for many African-American girls.

the limelight. They sported bouffant hair, along with dresses studded with sequins, rhinestones, and pearls. These dresses were so elaborately decorated that a single dress weighed as much as 30 pounds (14 kg).[6] The decision to dress so glamorously was, according to Supremes member Mary Wilson, a conscious decision. The group wanted to show their audiences that despite coming from poor backgrounds, they had become successful African-American women.

The social, economic, and political upheaval of the 1960s can be seen in the way women's fashions evolved during the decade. Women began the decade wearing housedresses and working as housewives. Many women ended the decade in miniskirts and working outside of the home. This decade brought women new freedoms and fashions and prepared them for the exciting years to come.

Makeup Reflects *Social Change*

Trends in fashion and cosmetics often reflect the social attitudes of the times. In the 1950s and early 1960s, women wore makeup that made them look soft and feminine. Popular trends centered on arched eyebrows, bright lips, delicate eyes, and even skin tones created with heavily applied makeup. This style of makeup coincided with the restrictive gender stereotypes that kept women in the home.

1950s makeup

1960s makeup

As the feminist movement began to change the way women perceived their role in society, makeup and fashion also changed. Instead of applying makeup to look soft and dainty, young women in the 1960s used it to achieve a striking appearance. They used heavy eyeliner and false lashes to make their eyes look large. Soft, pale lips made the eyes stand out even more. This trend showed the world that women were taking charge of their own appearance and that they were not afraid to be bold.

Joni Mitchell introduced a new
style in the 1970s.

CHAPTER SIX

Style Evolves in the 1970s and 1980s

I n the early 1970s, folk musician Joni Mitchell worked her way into the record collections and wardrobes of millions of US women. Her long hair, tie-dyed dresses, funky jewelry, and bare feet marked a drastic departure from the mod styles worn by sixties stars.

Mitchell embraced a style of originality and comfort. Many women welcomed this new, relaxed style of dress. It fit well into the liberation movements that came to dominate the cultural climate of the 1970s, and it allowed women to express their individuality by wearing homemade, vintage, or repurposed clothing.

Decades of Turmoil and Growth

The 1970s were an exciting and turbulent decade. The progressive movements that began in the 1960s, such as civil rights and women's liberation, continued to gain momentum during the 1970s. Women finally gained access to prestigious schools, such as Harvard and Dartmouth. The environmental movement was born, and the first Earth Day was celebrated in 1970. However, this decade saw crises as well. President Richard Nixon resigned from office in shame after a political scandal. An oil crisis and economic recession made many Americans worry about their futures.

By the beginning of the 1980s, many Americans were tired of the scandals, revolutionary spirit, and economic troubles of the previous decade. Americans grew more conservative and enjoyed an economic boom. The "yuppie" was born. This was a young, well-paid, and well-educated professional living in an urban area. More women entered the workplace, and they enjoyed a wider range of career options than ever before. In 1960, just 9 percent of women worked in banking and financial management. By 1983, that number had soared to 39 percent.[1] Women saw more opportunities in blue-collar work too. Women flooded the workplace as butchers, bartenders, and other jobs that were previously considered appropriate only for men.

Women Take Charge

The changes in society and the progress made by the feminist movement changed the way women dressed. Women began wearing clothing that was more functional, comfortable, and appropriate for long workdays. Department store Sears, Roebuck and Company even developed a line of clothing with strong zippers, durable fabric, and big pockets for women working in blue-collar jobs.

Females found leadership positions in many parts of the business world, including the fashion industry. Bethann Hardison, for example, left her career as a successful model to found her own talent agency that focused on representing women of color. Designers such as Laura Ashley and Diane von Furstenberg built fashion empires that brought in millions of dollars in profit.

While some women were busy gaining ground in the high-profile fashion world, others were busy strutting their styles in the underground punk rock scene. These rockers favored leather jackets, ripped jeans, electric colored hair, and rough accessories such as studded collars and safety pins. Both men and women often wore chunky boots, band

Women moving into corporate jobs in the 1970s chose to wear more conservative outfits.

T-shirts, and leather jewelry. Some even shaved the sides of their heads and styled the middle into a tall crest called a mohawk. Punk style was not for the lighthearted.

Diane von Furstenberg's Wrap Dress

Many women working in the fashion industry were influenced by the cultural shifts occurring at the time, including the feminist movement and the new role of women in the workplace. One designer who created fashions specifically for the evolving role of women was Diane von Furstenberg. She set out to create a dress that would flatter all bodies without needing to be altered. In 1974, she made a comfortable wrap dress out of stretchy jersey fabric. It was an instant hit. Women started to associate the dress with female power and independence. It was great for work, weekends, or nightlife. It represented democratic values because it fit every woman. And a woman created it.

Furstenberg sold more than one million of her innovative wrap dresses in just two years.[2] Her design house thrived as she created other comfortable and versatile garments. Before long,

Furstenberg became a pillar of the fashion industry. Today, the wrap dress is a must-have garment for professional women. Furstenberg's business has continued to grow. Her clothes are sold in more than 55 countries, and Forbes named her one of the 20 Most Powerful Women in Business in 2012.[4]

Laura Ashley's Romantic Styles

Not all designers focused on dressing women for the workplace. Laura Ashley created clothing that was reminiscent of times gone by. Her floral, soft, feminine fabrics and flowing dresses looked as if they would fit better in a country cottage than in a corner office. Though her clothes did not focus on the new freedoms women were enjoying, Ashley's designs still reflected

Von Furstenberg appears in one of her iconic wrap dresses after a runway show.

the feminist movement of the time. She used her clothing to rebel against the sexy and revealing trends of the 1960s. Many feminists thought 1960s styles such as miniskirts were created to please men. Ashley's garments were a reaction against these styles.

Ashley created a fashion and lifestyle empire before her death in 1985. The company created home goods, fashions, and accessories. Today, the design house continues to earn profits selling clothing for women and children, as well as home furnishings.

Rei Kawakubo Pushes Boundaries

In the 1980s, women designers continued to push boundaries as they found creative expression in unique and daring designs. Rei Kawakubo became an international fashion star in the early 1980s with her groundbreaking designs. Rather than design body-hugging or revealing clothing, she used large amounts of fabric to create huge, voluminous garments that disguised a woman's shape. One of her most notable collections earned the nickname the Quasimodo collection after the character in *The Hunchback of Notre Dame* due to the large bumps of fabric she sewed into the clothing. Kawakubo purposefully used her clothing to make a woman's body look different, even disfigured. By doing so, she raised awareness of the expectations of how a woman's body should look. Her clothing was often so unusual that assistants in her shops had to actually show customers how to put garments on. Despite their unusual appearance, women loved Kawakubo's clothing. The garments were comfortable and unique, and women could style them in many different ways to make them feel personalized.

BETHANN HARDISON

Bethann Hardison was a successful model living in New York City in the 1970s. She appeared in magazines such as *Allure, Vogue,* and *Harper's Bazaar.* These achievements were made even more significant by the fact that Hardison was African American. Much of the fashion world was still closed to African-American models at the time, and along with models such as Iman and Beverly Johnson, Hardison was proud to break down these racial barriers.

In 1981, she decided to make a career change. She quit modeling and began working as an activist, focusing on helping more African-American models find success in the fashion industry. In 1984, she founded the Bethann Management Agency, which focused on bringing racial diversity into fashion modeling. Four years later, she cofounded the Black Girls Coalition, an organization that advocates for African-American models' rights. Hardison's work has resulted in more and more African Americans being featured in magazines, runway shows, and television shows.

Working under the label Comme des Garçons (French for "like boys"), Kawakubo proved herself to be a brilliant businesswoman whose success has lasted long past the 1980s. She is credited with inventing the pop-up shop. In 2004, she started opening temporary clothing stores in cities around the world. Instead of becoming permanent locations, her pop-up shops were intended to last only a

A model walks the runway wearing one of Kawakubo's designs.

very short time. These stores created buzz around Kawakubo's clothing and made consumers feel an urgent need to shop at her stores before they closed. In addition to her pop-up shops and runway collections, Kawakubo also created affordable lines of clothing for retailers such as H&M. In this way, she assured that her clothing made its way into all parts of society. Wealthy people able to afford haute couture, middle-class department store shoppers, and fashion-forward trend hunters who followed her pop-up shops could all wear Kawakubo's designs.

Years of Empowerment and Expression

Women's fashions in the 1970s and 1980s were constantly changing. Trends fluctuated from bellbottoms and polyester to power suits and exercise wear. Women utilized fashion as a way to express themselves and assert their economic and professional power. And more than ever, the fashions they were wearing were designed by women.

Women emerged from these years with more authority, greater equality in the workplace, and a vision for what they wanted in the future. The fashions they wore reflected their evolving role in society. Women's wardrobes included more types of clothing to fit the new, diverse place they occupied in the world.

POWER SUITS

Women began wearing suits in the 1920s, with Coco Chanel's matching collarless jackets and fitted skirts. However, this garment did not come to represent power and authority until the 1980s, when it coincided with the flood of women into the professional workplace. These suits usually consisted of a boxy jacket with big shoulder pads and a straight skirt or slacks. They did not shape to a woman's body. Instead, they made her appear larger and more imposing. The 1988 movie *Working Girl* brought power suits into the limelight, as Melanie Griffith's character advances from lowly secretary with a bad wardrobe to executive powerhouse in a matching power suit.

As women gained more equality and freedom in the workplace, the power suit slowly fell out of popularity. By the early 1990s, women's work wardrobes included softer fabrics and body-conscious silhouettes. It seemed as though they no longer needed their clothing to show that they were capable of getting their jobs done.

MTV Makes Musicians
into Fashion Stars

On August 1, 1981, a groundbreaking television station called MTV burst onto the airwaves. This channel showed music videos 24 hours a day, every day. It was aimed at teenagers who were interested in listening to new music. It was an enormous success, not only in broadcasting new music to teens around the world, but also in influencing the way they dressed.

Stars such as Madonna and Cyndi Lauper had been creating great music before the birth of MTV, but few people had been able to watch them perform. MTV gave artists the chance to add a visual component to their music. The clothing they wore in their videos soon sparked fashion trends around the world.

One of the most influential artists was Madonna, who earned the nickname the Material Girl after her hit song and outlandish fashions. Her videos have been credited with starting many iconic 1980s fashion trends, such as neon colors, white lace and pearls, and stacks of bright bangle bracelets.

MTV opened up a new way for viewers around the world to see fashion trends on musicians such as Madonna.

Claire Danes's character helped to inspire the 1990s grunge trend.

CHAPTER SEVEN

The Catwalk Rules in the 1990s

After its start in the 1980s, MTV continued to impact teen style in the 1990s with music videos and award shows. But one of the biggest influences on teen wardrobes was *My So-Called Life*, a TV drama that aired on MTV. Claire Danes starred as Angela Chase, an awkward and uncertain teen. Unlike the stars on other network shows, Chase did not appear in bright, clean, perfect outfits. Her on-screen wardrobe reflected her troubled and rebellious personality. She often wore slouchy jeans, flannel shirts, and chunky combat boots. Her style reflected the popular musical genre of the time that was known as grunge. Artists in the grunge movement played harsh and heavy melodies and often wore clothing that looked old and tattered.

Chase's wardrobe captured the spirit of American teens. It was grungy and rebellious, yet it was also comfortable and easy to wear. It contributed to the global trend of oversized flannel shirts that came to define much of 1990s fashion.

Life in the 1990s

The 1990s have often been called "the best decade ever."[1] The US economy was booming, violent crime rates were falling, and artistic culture was thriving. Bands such as Nirvana were topping the charts, and the Harry Potter books were favorite choices for readers around the world. *New York Times* writer Kurt Anderson called the 1990s "the happiest decade of our American lifetimes."[2]

For women in fashion, the 1990s were a time for money, fame, and occasionally scandal. Designers and models were earning more money and gaining access to more power than ever before. Occasionally this fame became troublesome, as high-profile fashion figures were forced to deal with personal problems in the limelight. The catwalk emerged as the center stage for fashion. Runway shows became high-profile events. They featured glamorous models strutting new styles in front of eager fashion professionals, celebrities, and journalists.

While the 1990s brought some women fortune, this decade

JENNIFER ANISTON AND "THE RACHEL"

One of the biggest fashion trends in the 1990s was a haircut nicknamed the Rachel after Jennifer Aniston's character on the hit sitcom *Friends*. *Elle* magazine even reported that the layered bob "singlehandedly defined a generation."[3] Aniston might have been the inspiration for millions, but she was not a fan of the look. "I think it was the ugliest haircut I've ever seen," she later recalled.[4]

also saw many women in fashion struggle. Models publicly dealt with issues surrounding drug use, eating disorders, and body image. Designers struggled to balance family life with their careers. And the media was suddenly interested in covering every juicy detail.

Female designers flooded the fashion industry in the 1990s. They came from different backgrounds and brought unique perspectives to the runway. Some of these women focused on fun, flirty, and sexualized clothes. Others were sophisticated and glamorous. Still others bent gender norms by dressing women in masculine styles.

INVASION OF THE SUPERMODELS

In the late 1980s, the supermodel was born. These models appeared in movies, television commercials, print campaigns, and more. For the first time since Twiggy rocked the 1960s, models were celebrities. Christie Brinkley and Elle Macpherson were some of the late 1980s' most successful supermodels.

By the early 1990s, supermodels had become super celebrities. Cindy Crawford, Linda Evangelista, Naomi Campbell, Christy Turlington, and a few other select models enjoyed unprecedented success. They went on talk shows, were speculated about in gossip magazines, and appeared in blockbuster films. They were famous for being beautiful, powerful, and extremely well paid. In 1990, Evangelista told *Vogue* magazine about supermodels' excessive paychecks: "We don't wake up for less than $10,000 a day."[5]

Vivienne Westwood's Historic Styles

In the 1970s and 1980s, self-taught designer Vivienne Westwood was famous in the London punk rock fashion scene. She opened a boutique to sell her designs, and it soon became a popular meeting place for fashion-forward musicians and artists. In the early 1990s, Westwood moved on from the

Westwood's designs are playful and loud,
a change from many designers.

punk scene and began experimenting with other styles. Her collections featured a wide variety of themes, including shirts inspired by pirates and sweaters decorated in computer game patterns. She playfully combined historically inspired pieces with sexually suggestive silhouettes, cuts, and motifs, such as short ballerina skirts and English hunting costumes.

Westwood's work is praised by celebrities, journalists, and even the Queen of England, who gave the designer an Officer of the Most Excellent Order of the British Empire award in 1993. Westwood earned notoriety after supermodel Naomi Campbell famously fell while wearing a pair of the designer's 9-inch (23 cm) blue mock-crocodile heels on the runway. Westwood's design house continues to thrive today. It sells clothing and accessories for men and women.

Betsey Johnson's Offbeat Style

Betsey Johnson is another designer who found her foothold in the fashion industry during the wild days of punk rock before skyrocketing to fashion fame in the 1990s. She crafted bright, fun, and affordable clothes for young and trendy fashion lovers. Most of her clothing could be purchased for around $150, which was much less than other designers at the time.[6] Customers flocked to her store in the SoHo neighborhood of New York City for her flowing fabrics, sexy silhouettes, and quirky details. In the early 1990s, she added swimwear and shoes to her fashion line. Soon after, she added a tailored men's line.

Johnson's fun designs continue to be popular today.

Customers loved Johnson's style, and also the personality she projected to the public. Johnson even grew famous for doing cartwheels at the end of her fashion shows.

Johnson's bold sense of style and youthful demeanor has made her a powerful presence in the fashion industry. In 1999, she earned the Council of Fashion Designers of America's coveted Timeless Talent Award.

A Designer Balances Work and Family

While Betsey Johnson was cartwheeling down the catwalk, designer Donna Karan was busy juggling her marriage, her children, and a fashion empire. Karan got her start working under another influential female fashion designer, Anne Klein. When Klein became sick from breast cancer, Karan took over the business, despite having a newborn baby to care for. From early on in her career, Karan proved that she could juggle life as a wife, mother, and businesswoman. This is a challenging balancing act for many women in fashion.

After working at Anne Klein, Karan started her own fashion label called Donna Karan in 1984. It focused on the idea that women only needed "seven easy pieces" of clothing to form a complete wardrobe.[7] They were interchangeable and could be worn to brunch, to business meetings, or on vacation. This label was so successful that Karan started a more affordable label called DKNY in 1989. By the early 1990s, Karan was one of the world's biggest fashion designers. Celebrities loved her styles, and some of her dresses even earned pop culture nicknames. For example, when First Lady Hillary Clinton wore a Donna Karan black dress with open shoulders to a White House dinner, the press called it "the cold shoulder dress."[8] Copies of the dress soon popped up at boutiques around the country. By the late 1990s, Karan expanded her fashion empire to include menswear, children's clothing, skin care, eyewear, and even perfume. Her business sense and taste in fashion proved that she was a force to be reckoned with.

Female Style in the 1990s

The fashion industry was bountiful ground for female designers in the 1990s. Dozens of women achieved fame and fortune by creating unique, comfortable, and beautiful clothing. Klein, Karan, Westwood, Johnson, and many others became household names. Shoppers recognized their labels at department stores, and viewers heard

Karan's multiple businesses are still thriving today.

their brands mentioned on televised red carpets. More than ever before, women were molding the fashion world.

Female designers were not the only women who were changing the landscape of the fashion industry. Musicians, actresses, athletes, and other high-profile women were influencing the way people dressed by wearing interesting wardrobes for their performances or out in public. Olympic sprinter Florence Griffith Joyner, known as FloJo, brought outrageously long fingernails and outlandish makeup onto the track and into the spotlight. Courtney Love highlighted grunge fashion in her performances as the lead singer for the band Hole. Along with her famous husband, Kurt Cobain, Love made flannel shirts and heavy boots a pervasive fashion trend among young people in the 1990s.

The end of the 1900s marked a substantial shift in the role women played in fashion. They started the century as muses, models, and very occasionally as designers. But after 100 years, women were everywhere in the fashion industry. From models to designers,

HOLLYWOOD DARLINGS DEFINE STYLE

Two of the decade's greatest fashion influences were Hollywood sweethearts Drew Barrymore and Winona Ryder. These actresses enjoyed enormous success on-screen in films such as Barrymore's *The Wedding Singer,* and Ryder's *Edward Scissorhands.*

Barrymore was known for fashioning her own style from grunge, bohemian, and girly elements. Her short blonde hair, thin eyebrows, and dark lipstick became iconic trends of the decade. Ryder had a darker style that combined dark colors, grunge, and girly elements. The petite actress was famous for her simple yet elegant red carpet looks.

fashion photographers to fashion journalists, fashion illustrators to apparel buyers at major department stores, women were influencing every corner of the industry.

MUSICIAN STYLE

Female musicians spanned a wide range of styles in the 1990s. On one end of the extreme were grunge musicians such as Courtney Love of Hole, Nina Gordon of Veruca Salt, and D'arcy Wretzky of the Smashing Pumpkins. These rockers combined baby doll dresses and oversized flannel shirts with combat boots to achieve a tough, dark, and world-weary look.

On the other end of the spectrum, the princesses of pop music wore styles that were bright, cheery, and provocatively tight. Britney Spears, Christina Aguilera, and Jessica Simpson appeared in chart-topping music videos in pastel crop tops, low-slung jeans, and bubble gum–colored accessories. Unlike the women of grunge, these singers were polished and heavily produced, and their wardrobes were carefully constructed to have mass appeal.

Kate Moss
and Thin Models

In 1993, Calvin Klein cast British model Kate Moss in his ad campaign. The 18-year-old model did not look similar to the healthy, vibrant models people were used to seeing. Instead, she was pale, extremely thin, and childlike. The ads were controversial, but they also made Moss an instant celebrity. Soon, designers began looking for other models who looked similar to Moss.

This trend in fashion coincided with the rise in popularity of the street drug heroin. People who used heroin often lost large amounts of weight and became pale. Critics pointed at the similarities between some of the industry's top models and the victims of drug addiction. They said the fashion industry was glamorizing an unhealthy lifestyle. Others worried it would encourage young women to develop eating disorders.

Moss has long denied ever having done heroin or having an eating disorder. She claims that she was simply naturally thin, and her grueling work schedule gave her the famous appearance.

Moss has worked in fashion for more than 20 years.

Moss walks the runway for a Calvin Klein
show in June 1993.

Patricia Field is credited with bringing designer fashion into the homes of millions of viewers of *Sex and the City*.

CHAPTER EIGHT

Fashion of the 2000s

H BO's hit show *Sex and the City* defined fashion for women in the early 2000s. Viewers eagerly tuned in each week to check out the dresses, hats, purses, and shoes the four stars paraded across the screen. The brain behind the fashion was legendary wardrobe designer Patricia Field.

Field's on-screen styles impacted the way a generation of women dressed. She brought designer names such as Manolo Blahnik and Prada out of the upper levels of society and into the vocabulary of everyday women. In addition to owning a boutique that has been a fashion landmark for more than 50 years, Field has worked in television and film for decades.

Life in the 2000s

Life in the early 2000s was fast-paced and ruled by new technologies. These years saw the invention of the iPhone, Wikipedia, and US hybrid cars, among countless other digital innovations. The Internet made global communication and commerce instantly accessible. This decade was also heavily influenced by violence and war. The terror attacks of September 11, 2001, followed by the War in Afghanistan (2001–2014) and the Iraq War (2003–2011) shaped the way people felt about religion, national identity, and security.

Fashion reflected these cultural phenomena. Clothing adapted to incorporate technical advancements as well as to reflect the militaristic climate. iPhone-sized pockets began appearing in jackets and pants, allowing wearers to keep these handy gadgets close at hand at all times. Military-inspired colors and patterns, such as olive and camouflage, also became popular trends in fashion for both men and women.

FASHION AND THE INTERNET

In the early 2000s, the Internet changed the way people shopped. Consumers were no longer limited to local stores or catalogs. Suddenly, they could buy apparel from boutiques or designers located around the world. This drastically changed the climate of fashion sales. Internet retail sites, known as E-tail, began popping up to cater to all sorts of customers. Women are playing a vital role in the growing sector of fashion E-tail. Female entrepreneurs have created successful online shopping sites such as Gilt.com, OneKingsLane.com, and RenttheRunway.com.

Leaders of the Industry

Women continued to impact the fashion industry during the early 2000s through their creative design. New female designers appeared, and some female powerhouses of the previous years continued to achieve success on the catwalk and in retail. Some female designers continued to work after two and even three decades. Karan, von Furstenberg, Hulanicki, Johnson, and Westwood were among this group of designers whose work continued to sell around the world.

Women also achieved new levels of success through their business expertise. Women attained more executive positions in apparel companies than ever before. Sharen Jester Turney became the president and CEO of apparel giant Victoria's Secret in 2006. Marka Hansen worked as president of Gap Inc. from 2007 to 2011, achieving great strides for the popular retailer. Kay Krill, president and CEO of clothing store Ann Taylor, earned the title "one of the most powerful women in New York" for the incredible success she has achieved

Turney after the 2015 Victoria's Secret Fashion Show

for the popular retailer. Under her management, the company became a $1 billion business.[1]

Despite the progress these business pioneers made, women were still very underrepresented in the executive management of apparel brands. None of the top 15 apparel companies in the Forbes 500 list had female CEOs.[2] Even though women exerted overwhelming influence in the industry, it was clear they still had room to grow professionally.

This decade also saw women make strides in diversifying the overwhelmingly Caucasian industry. Constance White was an extremely successful African-American journalist, style editor, and television correspondent in the early 2000s. She wrote for the *New York Times* style section, became the fashion editor at *Elle*, and even became the style director of online giant eBay. Robin Givhan is an African-American fashion journalist for publications such as *Newsweek* and the *Washington Post*. She became the first writer ever to earn a Pulitzer Prize for fashion journalism.[3] Her Pulitzer was awarded for her many essays that combined fashion criticism with social and cultural criticism. Somali-born former model Iman also saw great successes during the 2000s. After retiring from modeling, Iman started her own cosmetics line that catered to women of color. It was incredibly profitable, and Iman soon partnered with cosmetics giant Procter & Gamble in order to keep up with the demand. Iman went on to appear on television shows, such as *The Fashion Show* and Canada's *Project Runway*. She also founded her own line of handbags and jewelry. These women beat the odds to bring diversity into the industry and helped pave the way for women of color in the future.

Bridal Style and Everyday Glamour

Vera Wang was another woman of color to change the landscape of fashion in the 2000s. She started her career in fashion journalism. She worked as a fashion editor at *Vogue* magazine for 15 years before working as an accessories designer at Ralph Lauren. When it was time for her 1989 wedding, she decided to design her own dress. She sketched a design and worked with a tailor to craft a beautiful and elaborate gown. In 1990, Wang opened her own bridal boutique. At first, Wang stocked other

Wang's brand eventually grew to include everyday clothing.

designers' dresses, but soon she began making and selling her own designs. Within a decade, Wang had become a bridal enterprise. Her business was worth an estimated $80 million.[6]

Wang spent the early 2000s fortifying her fashion empire. She worked with her design team to create custom, beautiful wedding dresses for her wealthy clients. Fashion insiders estimate Wang was selling more than 10,000 custom wedding dresses per year. Each of these gowns cost between $2,000 and $30,000 and took hundreds of hours to create.[7] Her attention to detail and modern design style made her a favorite of celebrities and other high-profile brides.

Though the Vera Wang brand continues to focus on wedding gowns, Wang spent the 2000s expanding her brand to include other designed goods. By the end of the decade, Vera Wang sold accessories, fragrances, eyewear, evening gowns, and home goods.

Chloé, Céline, and Motherhood

As women of color achieved new levels of success in fashion, another group of women was struggling to fit in: mothers. Phoebe Philo was a leader in her industry who worked hard to establish a place for motherhood in fashion.

Philo started her career working for designer Stella McCartney at the fashion house Chloé. Within four years, she was promoted to creative director for the successful fashion brand. After achieving great success at Chloé, Philo moved to the French brand Céline, where her work was internationally praised. She earned the title British Designer of the Year in 2004 and again in 2010. Philo was well-known for her modern, understated designs and fresh approach to functional fashion. But she became famous for the way she handled becoming a mother.

Unlike women designers of the past, who had struggled to juggle their fashion careers with raising their children, Philo became the first well-known designer to take maternity leave after the birth of each of her three children. The executives at Chloé and Céline did not punish Philo for this decision. In fact, they reorganized their businesses to allow for her to spend time with her family. For many in the industry, this was a promising sign that fashion corporations valued women and their many family obligations.

Anna Wintour, *center*, is a staple at fashion shows.

Anna Wintour Shapes Fashion

Vogue is one of the most well-known fashion magazines in the industry. But when Anna Wintour became the editor in chief of *Vogue* in 1988, the publication was struggling. Within years, Wintour transformed the magazine into a thriving journal for high-end fashion, society, and philanthropy. Wintour also worked hard to support other professionals in the industry she believed in. She featured promising up-and-coming photographers, designers, and models in *Vogue*. Many credit Wintour with helping them start their careers. Wintour even helped create the Council of Fashion Designers/Vogue Fashion Fund, an organization that gives young designers financial support as they build their businesses.

Wintour believed *Vogue* could have an important impact on the world. She used it to highlight interesting fashions, but also to give powerful women a platform to share their stories. She featured politicians and philanthropists on the cover.

Wintour used her influence to effect change in the world. Like so many other females in the fashion industry at the time, she realized she could change the way people saw women in fashion. As the early 2000s transitioned into the next decade, women in all areas of the fashion industry stood on the shoulders of pioneers such as Wintour to reach higher, achieve more, and create art in fashion.

ECO-FRIENDLY FASHION

The fashion industry can contribute to environmental problems, such as pollution, the depletion of natural resources, and climate change. Some designers have decided to create eco-friendly fashions that are better for the earth. These designers try to produce, ship, and sell their fashions in ways that are not wasteful. They use a variety of methods to create low-impact fashions, such as reusing vintage fabric and using local suppliers to cut down on the need for transportation.

Tara St. James is one designer who creates sustainable clothes for her label Studio NY in Brooklyn, New York. She tries to use patterns that create little to no fabric waste, and she also uses organic and recycled fabrics.

Major fashion label Stella McCartney is also striving to produce clothing in an eco-friendly fashion. The design house uses organic fabrics whenever possible and also uses recycled materials in its clothing. Stella McCartney stores even strive to use low-energy light bulbs to cut down on the electricity they use.

Expensive designer brands teaming up with stores such as Target help make these designs more accessible to a larger group of consumers.

CHAPTER NINE

Fashion of the Future

I n the early 1900s, a small handful of talented female fashion entrepreneurs defied the odds to become not just artists, but also businesswomen in an industry dominated by men. Today, the fashion industry looks very different. Women around the globe are found in all areas of the business, including design, photography, journalism, and modeling. Though they still do not occupy a majority in the industry, the number of women working in fashion is growing each year.

The role fashion plays in society is changing. Rather than simply a pursuit for the very wealthy and clothing-inclined, fashion is becoming a medium of self-expression for people from a wider range of economic classes. High-end fashion designers are creating affordable department store collections in addition to their existing haute couture lines. This means the price for their designs has an extremely wide range. For example, a dress from Italian design label Missoni can cost approximately $1,900. But a Missoni dress designed for popular retailer Target is only $40.[1] This shift in fashion has had a democratizing effect on the industry. And many women designers have been pioneers in this shift. Lilly Pulitzer, Jil Sander, and Stella McCartney have all created low-cost collections for retailers such as Gap and Target.

In addition to designing clothing for a wider range of price levels, women are also working hard to create clothing that appeals to a diverse group of shoppers with different body types. Two of the biggest plus size retailers, J. Jill and Torrid for Hot Topic, are run by female CEOs. A female president runs Allistyle, an inclusive fashion brand that caters to women of all shapes and sizes. This innovative brand aims to make all shoppers feel valued and welcomed, regardless of their size.

MAKING HISTORY MODERN

When Angela Ahrendts joined British brand Burberry as CEO in 2006, the company was in trouble. The aging luxury brand had been a staple for quality necessities among English people for more than 150 years. In fact, British soldiers even wore Burberry coats in the trenches during World War I. However, the brand needed a new vision for the new millennium. Burberry stores around the world were all selling different products, such as dog collars in Hong Kong and kilts in London. The brand needed to be unified and revitalized. And Ahrendts was the right person for the job. In just six years, she doubled the company's profits by focusing on the company's strongest-selling products and unifying the label's design. She brought attention to Burberry's most famous product, the trench coat, and made it the highlight of all of the company's collections. She made it glamorous and elite, and she made sure it featured in all of the stores. Burberry is now a luxury retail giant.

Fashion Gets Political

Women have historically used fashion to make statements, whether it was a young queen refusing to wear a fur cape to her wedding or a radical young singer insisting on wearing a men's suit for her performance. Today, fashion is playing a powerful role in politics. Some high-profile political women are using their wardrobes to bring attention to new designers. They are also using fashion to tell the world about their personalities.

First Lady Michelle Obama has become an advocate for some of her favorite designers. She famously wore a yellow lace dress designed by Cuban-born American Isabel Toledo to her husband's 2009 inauguration. The First Lady has also brought fashion entrepreneurs into the limelight. Obama enjoys shopping at the Ikram boutique in Chicago, Illinois, which is owned by Israeli-born American Ikram Goldman. Having the endorsement of the First Lady has helped designers and store owners grow their businesses.

Obama wearing an Isabel Toledo dress

Many celebrities rely on Zoe to style them and suggest fashionable clothing.

Stylists

Wardrobe stylists and fashion stylists are popular emerging careers in the fashion industry. These professionals work with clients to provide them with cutting-edge, flattering, and unique outfits for formal occasions such as red carpet appearances and casual outings such as brunch. Some of the most famous stylists are women.

Rachel Zoe started her career as a freelance stylist. In those early days, she created outfits for stars such as Britney Spears and Jessica Simpson and earned less than $20,000 per year. Today, her clients include dozens of A-list movie stars such as Anne Hathaway, who pay her more than $6,000 per day to dress them for outings and events.[2] Zoe has created a fashion empire, including her own television show, apparel and accessories lines, and a hit digital newsletter. In addition to all of this, Zoe is a mother to two children. She works hard to balance her career and family. She reminds women their clothing can be powerful. She thinks of fashion as a form of expression: "Style is a way to say who you are without having to speak."[3]

Fashion Gets Creative

Since the birth of MTV, musicians have influenced the wardrobes of their fans. This continues to be true today. Stars such as Taylor Swift, Selena Gomez, and Ariana Grande have all influenced fashion trends among young women. Older stars continue to shape the fashion world as well. Madonna, Faith Hill, and Tina Turner are still darlings of the fashion industry, inspiring older listeners to imitate their unique styles.

Today, perhaps more than ever before, women in music are wielding fashion as a means of artistic expression. Mainstream musicians such as Lady Gaga and Nicki Minaj have pushed the limits of fashion to express their artistic ideas. Lady Gaga famously wore a dress made from meat. She used her raw meat ensemble to tell

THE WOMEN BEHIND HOMEGROWN STYLE

Etsy is an e-commerce website that gives craftspeople a platform to sell their wares to customers around the world. Shoppers can turn to Etsy to look for items such as handmade dresses, jewelry, and shoes. This one-stop shop approach to buying and selling crafts has revolutionized the handmade fashion industry.

Etsy has been extremely popular among female crafters. Approximately 86 percent of the sellers on Etsy are women.[4] Many female fashion designers have started their own brands on Etsy before launching their own websites or brick-and-mortar stores. Starting on Etsy allowed them to earn money without having the expense of maintaining a shop or website. Etsy began in a New York apartment in 2005.

people to stand up for themselves: "If we don't fight for our rights, pretty soon we're going to have as much rights as the meat on our bones."[5] To raise awareness of her song "Roman Holiday," Nicki Minaj walked down the red carpet at the 2012 Grammys wearing a red robe and accompanied by a man dressed as the pope. The connection between her unusual date and her album was that the pope lives in the Vatican, which is found in Rome, Italy. Her controversial wardrobe choice made people question her motives and also brought the pop star into the limelight.

Effecting Change in the World

Today, women are helping to create a fashion industry that will lead to a better future. One designer who has used her success to help others is Tory Burch. After starting her successful fashion line in 2004, which brought ballet flats and bright patterns into wardrobes around the world, Burch expanded her business to include a foundation that helps women entrepreneurs. The Tory Burch Foundation helps to educate, fund, and guide women as they grow their own businesses.

BILLION-DOLLAR UNDERWEAR

In 2012, 41-year-old Sara Blakely became the youngest woman to become a self-made billionaire. She earned her fortune by creating the Spanx line of undergarments to help women look and feel better in their clothes. Spanx were tight garments that stretched over women's thighs and bellies to create a smooth foundation for clothing. Her innovative underwear was so successful, Blakely expanded her line to include jeans, bras, activewear, and more. Her brand's mission focuses on empowering women to "feel great about themselves and their potential."[6] Blakely's success has earned her global recognition as an innovator and savvy businesswoman. *Time* magazine even included her in its 2012 list of the 100 Most Influential People.[7]

Women are also working to highlight the social impact the fashion industry can have. More and more women are trying to make clothing that has a positive influence on the world. They are modeling, designing, creating, selling, and documenting styles that make people feel good about themselves. This is a departure from the industry's historical approach to fashion that made many women feel poorly about their appearances. Instead of idealizing unrealistic beauty standards, such as young, thin models, today's women in fashion are praising a variety of ages and body types. This new, inclusive approach to fashion is making the industry a friendlier place for people of all ages and sizes.

In the fashion world, it is impossible to predict what styles and trends will emerge next. But one thing is certain: whatever happens next in fashion, women will be there.

UP-AND-COMING DESIGNERS

Today, a new avenue for ambitious young designers offers a shot at fame and fortune: television. Shows such as *Project Runway* and *Launch My Line* give hopeful designers the chance at fame and fortune as they pit their talents against one another in clothing contests. Some of today's most promising up-and-coming female designers have come from these shows. Gretchen Jones, the winner of *Project Runway's* eighth season, now shows at New York Fashion Week and runs her own fashion label, Gretchen Jones NYC.

Timeline

1840
Queen Victoria weds Prince Albert wearing white, not the traditional red-colored dress.

1851
Amelia Bloomer suggests that women wear pants.

1911
The Triangle Shirtwaist fire kills 145, mostly poor female employees.

1912
Maison Vionnet opens in Paris, France.

1914
Caresse Crosby patents the bra.

1925
Coco Chanel creates her collarless women's suit.

1926
Coco Chanel creates her little black dress.

1927
Elsa Schiaparelli's fashion house begins influencing women around the world.

1939
The World's Fair in New York City is the place to spot new and influential fashion trends.

1941

People in England begin wearing civilian clothing 1941.

1950

Claire McCardell is awarded the Women's National Press Club award.

1966

Hulanicki receives a box of shrunken skirts from the manufacturer and the miniskirt is born.

1974

Diane von Furstenberg creates the wrap dress.

1990

Vera Wang opens her own bridal boutique.

1993

Kate Moss appears in an ad for Calvin Klein jeans.

2005

Etsy is founded in an apartment in Brooklyn, New York.

2009

Michelle Obama wears an Isabel Toledo dress to President Barack Obama's inauguration.

2012

Sara Blakely is the youngest woman to become a self-made billionaire.

2014

Jessica Simpson's business is valued at $1 billion.

Essential Facts

KEY PLAYERS

- Coco Chanel, a Parisian designer who was famous for designing the little black dress and the Chanel suit, and for creating her fragrance Chanel No. 5

- Mary Quant, a British designer who is credited with creating "the London look," a style of 1960s dressing that utilized miniskirts, tall boots, and bold colors

- Diane von Furstenberg, an American fashion designer who created a timeless wrap dress that is still sold today

- Donna Karan, an American designer who became well known for her "seven easy pieces" concept for women's wardrobes

- Vera Wang, an American designer who started out selling custom wedding dresses and then expanded her business into a fashion empire

- Anna Wintour, the editor in chief for *Vogue* magazine, who was one of the most influential women in fashion for nearly three decades

WOMEN IN THE FASHION INDUSTRY

In the 1910s and 1920s, most female fashion designers worked in Paris, France. Hollywood heavily influenced American fashion in the 1930s. As wars were fought across the world, fashion trends changed. During World War II and the Korean War, much of women's fashion became utilitarian. In the 1960s, the hub for mod fashion was London, England. Cities were not the only influences on fashion. Music stars and movie stars played a large role in influencing trends. Joni Mitchell heavily influenced fashion in the 1970s. In the 1980s, as women gained a foothold in the workforce, female fashion began to feature items such as the power suit. Television, music, and technology influenced 2000s fashion.

IMPACT ON SOCIETY

Women have had an enormous impact on fashion's history. Serving in a variety of roles, from model and muse to designer and business owner, women have shaped the growth of the fashion industry. Women have worked hard to gain new footholds in the business of fashion. They still do not have an equal presence in the executive management of fashion companies, but each year they are working to close the gap.

QUOTE

"Vain trifles as they seem, clothes have, they say, more important offices than to merely keep us warm. They change our view of the world and the world's view of us."
—*Virginia Woolf*

Glossary

AVANT-GARDE
New or experimental ideas, especially in the arts.

BIAS CUT
A style of clothing construction in which the fabric is cut across the grain, creating a diagonal line.

CHIFFON
A type of very light, sheer silk or nylon.

CORSET
A tight-fitting women's undergarment.

COUTURIER
A fashion designer who creates custom clothing for clients.

ERMINE
White fur historically used to trim ceremonial robes.

FLAPPER
A nickname given to fashionable women in the 1920s.

HAUTE COUTURE
High-quality handmade clothing created by leading fashion brands.

HEROIN
An addictive drug.

MILLINER
A person who makes women's hats.

MOURN
To express sadness after a death.

MUSLIN
A lightweight cotton cloth.

PRET-A-PORTER
Designer clothes that are sold ready to wear, as opposed to being custom created.

SUSTAINABLE
A practice that avoids depleting natural resources.

SWEATSHOP

A type of factory where manual laborers are employed for low pay and are forced to work long hours under poor conditions.

TROMPE L'OEIL

Visual illusion that makes a flat object appear to have three dimensions.

Additional Resources

SELECTED BIBLIOGRAPHY

Bates, Karen Grigsby. "The Look of Power: How Women Have Dressed for Success." *NPR*. NPR, 23 Oct. 2014. Web. 28 Jan. 2016.

English, Bonnie. *A Cultural History of Fashion in the 20th and 21st Centuries*. New York: Bloomsbury, 2013. Print.

Spivack, Emily. "The History of the Flapper, Parts 1–4." *Smithsonian.com*. Smithsonian.com, 5 Feb. 2013. Web. 28 Jan. 2016.

Stevenson, N. J. *Fashion: A Visual History from Regency & Romance to Retro & Revolution*. New York: St. Martin's, 2011. Print.

FURTHER READINGS

Barker, Nigel. *Models of Influence: 50 Women Who Reset the Course of Fashion*. New York: Harper, 2015. Print.

Rissman, Rebecca. *A History of Fashion*. Minneapolis, MN: Abdo, 2015. Print.

Rubin, Susan Goldman. *Hot Pink: The Life and Fashions of Elsa Schiaparelli*. New York: Abrams, 2015. Print.

WEBSITES

To learn more about Women's Lives in History, visit **booklinks.abdopublishing.com**. These links are routinely monitored and updated to provide the most current information available.

FOR MORE INFORMATION

For more information on this subject, contact or visit the following organizations:

Costume Institute at the Metropolitan Museum of Art
1000 Fifth Avenue
New York, NY 10028
212-535-7710
http://www.metmuseum.org/about-the-museum/museum-departments/
curatorial-departments/the-costume-institute
Head to this historic landmark to see iconic fashions from around the world.

Costumes and Textiles Exhibit at the Chicago History Museum
1601 North Clark Street
Chicago, IL 60614
312-642-4600
http://chicagohistory.org/research/aboutcollection/costumes
Check out the amazing fashions on display at this museum in the heart of Chicago, Illinois.

Source Notes

CHAPTER 1. MODERN FASHIONISTAS AND THEIR HISTORIC ROOTS

1. Kayleen Schaefer. "How Bloggers Make Money on Instagram." *HarpersBazaar*. Hearst Communications, 20 May 2015. Web. 15 Feb. 2016.

2. "Vogue Overview of Opportunities." *Vogue*. Conde Nast, n.d. Web. 15 Feb. 2016.

3. Suzannah Ramsdale. "'I Don't Do Fashion. I Am Fashion.'—The 50 Best Style Quotes of All Time." *MarieClaire*. Marie Claire, 4 Jan. 2016. Web. 15 Feb. 2016.

4. Michael Garval. "Cléo de Mérode's Postcard Stardom." *Nineteenth-Century Art Worldwide*. Nineteenth Century Art Worldwide, 2016. Web. 15 Feb. 2016.

5. "Cléo de Mérode." *Toulouse-Lautrec Paris & the Moulin Rouge*. The Museum of Modern Art, n.d. Web. 15 Feb. 2016.

6. Suzannah Ramsdale. "'I Don't Do Fashion. I Am Fashion.'—The 50 Best Style Quotes of All Time." *MarieClaire*. Marie Claire, 4 Jan. 2016. Web. 15 Feb. 2016.

7. Biography.com Editors. "Amelia Bloomer Biography." *Biography.com*. A&E Television Networks, n.d. Web. 15 Feb. 2016.

CHAPTER 2. NEW STYLES FOR A NEW WORLD

1. Elizabeth Flock. "Queen Victoria Was the First to Get Married in White." *WashingtonPost*. Washington Post, 29 Apr. 2011. Web. 15 Feb. 2016.

2. "The Fight for Women's Suffrage." *History*. A&E Television Networks, n.d. Web. 15 Feb. 2016.

3. "Fire Kills 145 at Triangle Shirtwaist Factory." *History*. A&E Television Networks, n.d. Web. 15 Feb. 2016.

4. Ibid.

5. Yvette Mahe. "History of Haute Couture: Jeanne Lanvin." *Fashion in Time*. History of Fashion, 5 Nov. 2011. Web. 15 Feb. 2016.

6. Pauline West. "Flapper Fashion—1920s Fashion History." *Fashion-Era*. Fashion-era.com, 2014. Web. 15 Feb. 2016.

7. Suzannah Ramsdale. "'I Don't Do Fashion. I Am Fashion.'—The 50 Best Style Quotes of All Time." *MarieClaire*. Marie Claire, 4 Jan. 2016. Web. 15 Feb. 2016.

CHAPTER 3. THE THRILLING 1930s

1. Rashna Wadia Richards. *Cinematic Flashes: Cinephilia and Classical Hollywood*. Bloomington, IN: Indiana University Press, 2013. Print. 105.

2. "Women's Dinner Dress." *Philadelphia Museum of Art*. Philadelphia Museum of Art, 2016. Web. 15 Feb. 2016.

3. Suzannah Ramsdale. "'I Don't Do Fashion. I Am Fashion.'—The 50 Best Style Quotes of All Time." *MarieClaire*. Marie Claire, 4 Jan. 2016. Web. 15 Feb. 2016.

4. Susan McMillan. "Elizabeth Arden's Maine Chance Spa Up for Sale." *Portland Press Herald*. MaineToday Media, 13 June 2014. Web. 15 Feb. 2016.

5. "Madeleine Vionnet." *Vionnet*. Vionnet.com, n.d. Web. 15 Feb. 2016.

6. Ibid.

CHAPTER 4. THE WAR YEARS

1. "World War II History." *History*. A&E Television Networks, n.d. Web. 15 Feb. 2016.

2. "Pop-over." *The Metropolitan Museum of Art*. The Metropolitan Museum of Art, 2016. Web. 15 Feb. 2016.

3. "Inflation Calculator." *Dollar Times*. DollarTimes. com, n.d. Web. 15 Feb. 2015.

4. "Betty Grable." *Encyclopedia.com*. The Gale Group, 2005. Web. 15 Feb. 2016.

5. Ibid.

6. Biography.com Editors. "Edith Head Biography." *Biography.com*. A&E Television Networks, n.d. Web. 15 Feb. 2015.

7. Amy Henderson. "How Katharine Hepburn Became a Fashion Icon." *Smithsonian.com*. Smithsonian.com, 12 May 2015. Web. 15 Feb. 2016.

8. Biography.com Editors. "Lucille Ball Biography." *Biography.com*. A&E Television Networks, n.d. Web. 15 Feb. 2016.

9. "Korean War." *History*. A&E Television Networks, n.d. Web. 15 Feb. 2016.

CHAPTER 5. THE STARTLING 1960s

1. Biography.com Editors. "Twiggy Biography." *Biography.com*. A&E Television Networks, n.d. Web. 15 Feb. 2016.

2. Terri White. "Warhol And His Women." *Stylist*. Stylist, 2016. Web. 15 Feb. 2015.

3. "Barbara Hulanicki and Biba." *Victoria and Albert Museum*. Victoria and Albert Museum, 2016. Web. 15 Feb. 2015.

4. "Title VII of the Civil Rights Act of 1964." US Equal Employment Opportunity Commission. USA.gov, n.d. Web. 15 Feb. 2016.

5. Biography.com Editors. "Mary Quant Biography." *Biography.com*. A&E Television Networks, n.d. Web. 15 Feb. 2016.

Source Notes Continued

6. Eric Wilson. "Reliving the Glamour of the Supremes." *New York Times*. New York Times Company, 12 Oct. 2012. Web. 15 Feb. 2016.

CHAPTER 6. STYLE EVOLVES IN THE 1970s AND 1980s

1. George Guilder. "Women in the Work Force." *Atlantic*. Atlantic Monthly Group, Sept. 1986. Web. 15 Feb. 2016.

2. Michaela Angela Davis. "Democracy in a Dress: Diane von Furstenberg's Wrap Dress Turns 40." *CNN*. Cable News Network, 12 Mar. 2014. Web. 15 Feb. 2016.

3. Curtis M. Wong. "Annie Lennox Sounds Off on Being a 'Gender Bender,' Her Gay Fan Base and More." *HuffPost Queer Voices*. HuffingtonPost.com, 25 Sept. 2014. Web. 15 Feb. 2016.

4. Michaela Angela Davis. "Democracy in a Dress: Diane von Furstenberg's Wrap Dress Turns 40." *CNN*. Cable News Network, 12 Mar. 2014. Web. 15 Feb. 2016.

5. "1981: Charles and Diana Marry." *BBC*. BBC, n.d. Web. 15 Feb. 2016.

CHAPTER 7. THE CATWALK RULES IN THE 1990s

1. Kurt Andersen. "The Best Decade Ever? The 1990s, Obviously." *New York Times*. New York Times Company, 6 Feb. 2015. Web. 15 Feb. 2016.

2. Ibid.

3. Megan Cahn. "Is This the 'Rachel' Haircut of 2015?" *Elle*. Hearst Communications, 2016. Web. 15 Feb. 2016.

4. Zach Johnson. "Jennifer Aniston: The 'Rachel' Was One of the Hardest Hairstyles to Maintain." *E!* E! Entertainment Television, 14 May 2014. Web. 15 Feb. 2016.

5. N. J. Stevenson. *Fashion: A Visual History from Regency & Romance to Retro & Revolution*. New York: St. Martin's, 2011. Print. 247.

6. Biography.com Editors. "Betsey Johnson Biography." *Biography.com*. A&E Television Networks, n.d. Web. 15 Feb. 2016.

7. "Donna Karan Facts." *YourDictionary*. LoveToKnow, 2016. Web. 15 Feb. 2016.

8. Ibid.

CHAPTER 8. FASHION OF THE 2000s

1. "Kay Krill, President and CEO of Ann Taylor." *More.* Meredith Corporation, 2016. Web. 15 Feb. 2016.

2. Theresa Avila. "Here's How Many Female CEOs Actually Run the Biggest Clothing Companies." *Style. Mic.* Mic, 30 Oct. 2015. Web. 15 Feb. 2016.

3. "Chic and In Charge: 10 African-American Fashion Executives." *Madame Noire.* Moguldom Media, 22 June 2011. Web. 15 Feb. 2016.

4. Kim Bhasin. "How Jessica Simpson Built a Billion-Dollar Fashion Empire." *BloombergBusiness.* Bloomberg, 6 Apr. 2015. Web. 15 Feb. 2016.

5. Biography.com Editors. "Miuccia Prada Biography." *Biography.com.* A&E Television Networks, n.d. Web. 15 Feb. 2016.

6. "Vera Wang." *Encyclopedia.com.* Cengage Learning, 2016. Web. 15 Feb. 2016.

7. Ibid.

CHAPTER 9. FASHION OF THE FUTURE

1. Charlotte Wilder. "This is Why the Internet Freaked Out About Lilly Pulitzer for Target." *Boston.com.* Boston Globe Media, 13 Jan. 2015. Web. 15 Feb. 2016.

2. Lynn Hirschberg. "Being Rachel Zoe." *New York Times Magazine.* New York Times Company, 16 Sept. 2007. Web. 15 Feb. 2016.

3. Suzannah Ramsdale. "'I Don't Do Fashion. I Am Fashion.'—The 50 Best Style Quotes of All Time." *MarieClaire.* Marie Claire, 4 Jan. 2016. Web. 15 Feb. 2016.

4. Valentina Zarya. "Meet the 86%: This is Why Most Etsy Sellers are Women." *Fortune.* Fortune, 2 Aug. 2015. Web. 15 Feb. 2016.

5. Jillian Mapes. "Lady Gaga Explains Her Meat Dress: 'It's No Disrespect.'" *Billboard.* Billboard, 13 Sept. 2010. Web. 15 Feb. 2016.

6. "Putting Your Butt on the Line Pays Off." *Spanx.* Spanx, 2016. Web. 15 Feb. 2016.

7. Ibid.

Index

About the Author

Rebecca Rissman is a nonfiction author and editor. She has written more than 200 books about history, science, and art. Her book *Shapes in Sports* earned a starred review from *Booklist*, and her series Animal Spikes and Spines received *Learning Magazine*'s 2013 Teachers Choice for Children's Books. Rissman studied fashion history as part of her master's degree in English Literature at Loyola University Chicago. She lives in Chicago, Illinois, with her husband and two daughters. She enjoys hiking, yoga, and cooking.